AI in Human Resources
Insights, Automation, and Personalization

Table of Contents

2.2. The Role of AI in Early HR Transformation

The prime motive behind AI's early adoption in HR was efficiency. HR departments are notorious for their administrative backend tasks, which are time-consuming yet essential. Machine learning and AI-driven automation tools found application in streamlining these processes, freeing HR professionals to concentrate on other critical tasks that contribute to strategic decision-making.

AI's initial capabilities were promptly realized with applications like resume parsing and automated responses. By doing the work of numerous employees in mere minutes, AI positioned itself as a vital entity in HR's growth and evolution.

2.3. Understanding AI's Role in Data Analysis

As AI evolved from its early days of mere automation, another facet of its potential began emerging - data analysis.

Human Resources tends to generate mountains of data, and AI has the capacity to sift through this information and identify patterns that humans may miss. It offers predictive analytics that can help forecast employee trends and behaviors, flag potential issues before they become significant problems, and even predict future hiring needs.

Using AI, HR departments can now utilize data to support decision-making, effectively marrying quantitative analysis with qualitative experiences to improve department efficiencies.

2.4. Personalizing the Employee Experience with AI

The final piece of the AI and HR puzzle lies in the personalization of the employee experience. AI's ability to facilitate contextual conversations and interactions allowed HR departments to offer personalized service to their employees. With chatbots, employees could get instantaneous, personalized information about their concerns or inquiries.

Moreover, workspace platforms powered by AI began predicting employee needs even before they articulated them, thereby aligning the available resources in alignment with the employees' expectations.

As AI continues to improve, it promises to further refine and redefine the HR department. However, despite AI's evident progress and potential, it also introduces a novel set of challenges related to reliance, ethics, and privacy.

2.5. The Challenges AI Brings to HR

The application of AI within HR is not without concerns. To start with, there is the reliance issue. What happens if the AI platform fails or develops a fault? Can businesses risk interruptions?

The ethical issues surrounding bias in AI decision-making is another critical area. Even though AI can streamline processes and sift through data effectively, it can also inadvertently reinforce existing biases if not correctly programmed.

Moreover, concerns around privacy rights and the use of employee data by AI systems are an ongoing conversation, which will need to be addressed with robust guidelines, laws, and regulations over time.

In conclusion, the dawn of AI in HR is a fascinating exploration of the possibilities technology brings to typical corporate functions. Its potential to automate, deliver insights, and personalize makes it an unavoidable trajectory for human resources. However, as with any powerful technology, the challenges it introduces will require careful consideration and proactive management.

Chapter 3. Unraveling the AI and HR Interface

Deep into the 21st century, the role played by Artificial Intelligence (AI) in revolutionizing the business space cannot be understated. In HR departments, AI's impact is sweeping across every process - from recruitment and employee development, to retention strategies and even routine administrative tasks. This change is revolutionary, pivotal even, as organizations strive to leverage AI to optimize HR functions.

3.1. Understanding the AI and HR Ensemble

Key to unlocking the potential of the AI-HR interface is understanding the basics of how these two function together. Simply put, AI in HR constitutes the use of machine learning algorithms and predictive analytics to enhance HR functions. To illustrate, imagine a time-consuming task such as sorting through stacks of job applications. AI can automate this task, sifting through applications and identifying top talents based on set parameters, all in a fraction of the time it would take a human to accomplish the same task.

AI is not limited to tasks of an administrative nature. Functions like employee engagement, training, and succession planning can all be enhanced with AI. Machine learning algorithms can analyze vast data points to predict employee behavior, helping to foster a healthier work ambiance by proactively addressing issues before they escalate.

3.2. The AiHR Digital Transformation

The digital transformation brought about by the amalgamation of AI and HR is rapidly reshaping the business landscape. But, how can an HR department begin this transformation? One possible starting point is by identifying areas where AI can have a significant impact. For instance, automation is a key application area for AI in HR. Consider routine HR tasks such as scheduling, payroll management, or benefits administration. These tasks, while vital, are time-consuming and susceptible to human error. AI can automate these tasks, enhancing efficiency while reducing the likelihood of errors.

Another area is employee engagement and talent development. AI can help identify potential leaders within an organization, devise customized development programs, and even predict future talent needs of the organization. Training programs can be personalized using AI to suit each individual's learning style and pace, thereby increasing overall productivity.

3.3. Harnessing AI for Data-Driven Insights

Data-driven insights are the backbone of any successful HR strategy. By deploying AI, HR departments can benefit from predictive analytics and machine learning algorithms to better understand their workforce. For instance, AI can be used to analyze employee performance data, detect patterns and predict future trends. This could be instrumental in strategic HR decision making, and can also help in predicting employee turnover, thereby enabling HR to act proactively.

Fostering more personalized HR experiences is another area where AI shines. AI-based programs can learn from past interactions, preferences, and feedback to create highly customized experiences for employees. Whether it's in recruiting, onboarding, employee development, or exit interviews, AI can help deliver a more personal touch, thereby increasing employee satisfaction.

3.4. Future Prospects of AiHR

The future of AI in HR seems promising, with new possibilities continuously emerging. From AI-powered HR chatbots that offer 24/7 employee support, to AI-driven prediction models that can anticipate future skill requirements, the potential applications are virtually limitless. However, it's essential to remember that while AI can bring abundant opportunities, it's still just a tool that needs to be used wisely. Embracing AI doesn't mean replacing humans in HR entirely; rather, it's about finding the right balance between human and machine.

In a world where HR departments are continuously stretched for time and resources, AI offers a pathway to more efficient and strategic functioning. Organizational leadership should adopt a proactive approach towards this technology, leveraging AI's capabilities to elevate HR contributions in driving business outcomes. Understanding AI and HR's integral interface is not just about moving with the times, but about positioning an organization for a future where technology leads the way.

Chapter 4. AI Impact: Driving Efficiency in HR

Artificial Intelligence (AI) has arrived onto the scene as a revolutionary force in the world of Human Resources (HR), driving significant efficiency and providing invaluable benefits. Incorporating AI can free HR professionals from the tedium of routine tasks, allowing them to focus on people-centered work and strategic planning pertaining to employee lifecycle, thus evoking a stronger, more productive, and positive work environment. Let's delve into the intricacies and advantages of AI's impact on HR, which is making waves across industries globally.

4.1. The Path of Automation in HR

A significant portion of HR's daily tasks includes repetitive and administrative duties such as data entry, scheduling, and managing the immense paperwork that comes with each employee. AI comes up triumphant in its ability to automate these mundane aspects.

Take applicant tracking systems (ATS) as an example. Every recruiter knows the pain of sifting through hundreds, if not thousands, of resumes for a single job opening. AI-powered ATS systems automate the process, scanning for keywords, and qualifications to shortlist applications. By letting machine learning processes loose on stacks of resumes, HR can drastically reduce the time spent on the initial screening process.

Similarly, repetitive processes like onboarding, training reminders, and survey distributions can be automated, freeing up HR managers to focus on tasks that require a more personalized human touch.

4.2. Leveraging AI for Analytics and Reporting

Data-driven decision making is the cornerstone of effective HR management. AI can transform the mountain of data HR has access to into powerful, insightful analytics.

Imagine having predictive analytics that can identify turnover risks, highlight skill gaps, or forecast recruitment needs. With machine learning algorithms, these are no longer beyond reach. They take a deep dive into historical and real-time data, learning patterns, and predicting trends. When coupled with HR's expertise, these analytics can guide everything from recruitment strategies to performance management.

Moreover, AI can help in periodic HR reporting, reducing the time taken to collect, compile and analyze information. It gives HR professionals time back in their schedules, and provides the company with timely updates that can be essential to strategic planning and forecasting.

4.3. Enhancing Employee Experience with AI

AI is not just about automation and analytics; it's about creating meaningful employee experiences as well. Chatbots, an application of AI, are used for employee engagement, answering routine questions, and freeing HR professionals from the task of responding to each query.

Artificial Intelligence can also drive tailored learning and professional development programs. Based on an employee's performance reviews, skill gaps, and stated goals, AI can recommend individualized learning resources, paths, and even modify the recommendations as the employee progresses.

4.4. The Role of AI in Performance Management

With its ability to process large volumes of data quickly and accurately, AI is well-suited to assist in the process of performance evaluation as well. It can offer unbiased, data-derived insights into employee performance, helping maintain objectivity through reviews and appraisals.

AI can also serve as a tool for continuous performance tracking. It enables HR to collect real-time data on various performance metrics, providing insights and trends that can trigger early intervention or rewards and recognition.

Efficiency is of paramount importance in HR, which drives the momentum of any company. AI, through automation, analytics, and personalization, is facilitating this in an unprecedented way. It is a catalyst, boosting HR out of routine administrative tasks and into strategic contributors to a company's success. Encouraging the adoption of AI in HR not only propels businesses to evolve but also paves the way for a smarter HR ecosystem, one where technology and human intuition blend seamlessly to create a truly differentiated and positive organizational environment.

While the journey to integrate AI within HR may be challenging, this transformative path holds many rewards that can revolutionize the way businesses function. Therefore, it is an expedition worth embarking upon. You are on the doorstep of a new era in human resources management, and AI is your ticket to leap forward. Embrace the intelligence of machines, but remembering the spirit remains intrinsically human.

Chapter 5. From Insight to Foresight: AI in Data Analysis

The modern world is saturated with data. Every click, purchase, and interaction from both inside and outside the office is being documented, contributing to an endless stream of raw, undigested information. To allow HR professionals to leverage this data to transform their function, businesses need to look towards AI and it's capacity for data analysis.

Understanding humans, their behaviors, their skills, and optimizing their productivity is at the heart of human resources. Data, in the hands of HR professionals, presents an exciting opportunity to gain insights never before accessible. However, when you consider the sheer volume of information businesses accumulate daily, this task can seem overwhelming. Here AI comes to aid; it can change insights into foresight.

5.1. Harnessing the Power of Data

Harnessing the potential of this data is no easy task due to its magnitude and complexity. But, thanks to advances in machine learning and artificial intelligence, the playing field has changed dramatically. AI applications can swiftly sift through daunting amounts of data to derive valuable patterns and powerful insights.

Traditional data analysis techniques are no match for AI's rigorous, quick, and comprehensive approach. It can spot trends, identify risks, and propose solutions in the flick of an eye, a feat unthinkable a few decades ago. This capability transforms HR's role, enabling a proactive approach where decisions are foresighted and not solely based on past data.

5.2. Predictive Analytics

A significant aspect of AI's role in data handling lies in predictive analytics. These models work by recognizing patterns within data and using the analysis to predict future outcomes. This predictive power can have far-reaching implications for organizations.

In the recruitment field, for instance, predictive models can use years of recruitment data to identify patterns that will help in forecasting the necessary skills for future positions. Not only does this help in creating more efficient training and development programs, but it also enables more strategic recruitments that align with the organization's goals.

The power of predictive analytics also extends to employee retention. Using data from exit interviews, job satisfaction surveys, and performance reviews, AI can predict which employees are at risk of leaving the company. This proactive approach allows managers to address issues before they escalate, thus improving retention rates.

5.3. Personalized Employee Experience

The use of AI in data analysis also promises a more tailored employee experience. A data-driven approach can better understand employee needs, wants, and patterns of behavior.

Today, AI can trawl through mountains of data to understand what incentives truly drive employees, what forms of communication they respond to best, or what type of work environment they thrive in. AI opens the door to an era of hyper-personalization, where everything from the hiring process to career development can be tailored to each employee.

The role of AI doesn't stop at identifying these variables — it can also leverage insights to design highly individualized learning and development plans, career advancement strategies, and strengthen employee engagement.

5.4. Systems and Processes Streamlining

AI's role extends to reshaping HR systems and processes. AI's ability to analyze vast data sets can identify areas that need improvement and propose solutions to streamline workflows, automation, and operations.

As AI continues to evolve, it can also provide smart suggestions for updating internal policies. Its capacity to analyze the impact of existing regulations can inform changes that lead to improved performance, engagement, and overall staff morale.

5.5. Conclusion

The power of AI in data analysis goes beyond merely optimizing efficiencies. By transforming raw data into insights, then foresight, AI can unleash a world of predictive capabilities that provides valuable strategic assets for HR professionals to adapt at the same pace as the business world around them.

AI stands to revolutionize HR's work, not by replacing human judgment but enhancing it, shaping HR departments into a proactive force ready to deal with the challenges of tomorrow. AI helps transform HR from a reactive function to a strategic partner in shaping the organization's future.

Chapter 6. Changing the Way HR Communicates: AI and Personalization

As the inscription of artificial intelligence (AI) into the daily conduct of HR tasks becomes more pronounced, one area vividly transforming is the way HR communicates. By offering streamlined systems, intelligent algorithms, and data-based insights, AI is effectively overhauling the traditional ways of HR interaction. The power of AI in enhancing personalized communication presents a beacon of hope for businesses struggling with unnecessary delays, misunderstandings, and loss of productivity in HR-related interactions.

6.1. Understanding Personalization in HR Communication

Personalization, in the context of HR communication, revolves around creating meaningful and individualized interactions that relay the required information or decision accurately. In the era before AI, most of such interactions were essentially human driven and susceptible to errors, bias, and inconsistencies.

AI systems that incorporate aspects of machine learning and natural language processing are becoming game-changers. These intelligent systems are capable of learning from past interaction data patterns, interpreting them, and employing the gained insights to drive similar future interactions. They foster a climate of improved, timely decision making, and delivery of services across the HR procession chain, from recruitment to employee engagement and performance management.

6.2. The Power of AI in Streamlining HR Communication

As businesses expand and employee numbers increase, maintaining clear, personal, and consistent communication becomes a complex challenge. Utilizing AI to this end brings about automation and semantic understanding, which takes a considerable load off the HR team.

AI, through chatbots and virtual assistants, has revolutionized HR communication by being available 24/7 to answer employee queries, assist in tasks like booking leave or finding HR policies, and eliminating the human lag time that can slow down processes.

Moreover, AI-powered HR platforms may now analyse sentiments and emotions in text-based conversations offering deeper insights into employee mood and morale. This analysis paves the way to more empathetic and emotionally sensitive HR communication, a cornerstone in building a supportive work environment.

6.3. AI in Recruitment Communication

When it comes to the recruitment process, AI has streamlined communications in numerous ways. Many companies are now using AI-driven systems for initial candidate screening, interview scheduling, maintaining candidate communication, and even interviewing with AI-based chatbot recruiters.

Such AI-led personalization is highly effective. These smart systems ensure a smoother candidate experience and save a lot of administrative time for recruiters. They also substantially reduce the turnaround time for candidate selection, bettering a company's chances of securing high caliber candidates.

6.4. AI in Employee Engagement and Retention

Retaining employees remains a persisting challenge for HR departments globally. With the integration of AI, the realm of employee engagement and retention has seen significant improvements. AI can predict employee churn by analyzing employee variables and behaviors.

These insights guide HR professionals in personalizing their interaction and interventions with each employee. They can curate specific programs to avoid any loss of employees to attrition. AI in communication fosters better HR interaction, creating a substantial impact on employee satisfaction, and in turn, retention.

6.5. AI in Performance Management

Performance management is an area where AI can make a significant contribution. AI can help optimize performance reviews by analyzing vast amounts of data to generate real-time reviews. This can foster clear, frequent, and fact-driven communication between managers and their teams.

This utilization of AI allows for the synchronization of goals, immediate feedback, and reinforcement. AI-driven communication in performance management ensures greater transparency and results in clearly defined roles and expectations, fostering a system of continuous growth and improvement.

6.6. The Ethical Considerations

Despite the abundance of opportunities AI presents within HR communication, it's crucial to not overlook ethical considerations. Data privacy, for instance, is a concern with AI-driven communication systems. If mishandled, it could lead to significant legal and reputation damages.

Also, HR professionals should be wary of over-dependence on AI, which may lead to automation bias. Personal touches and human intuition still play a significant role in HR, especially in situations requiring empathy, a nuanced understanding of individuals, and complex decision-making.

In conclusion, the future of HR communication is synonymous with the advancement of AI and how it will be used to make communication more personalized, efficient, and insightful. However, as businesses tread the path of AI-led HR communication, maintaining a balance between technology and personal human interaction will be key in ensuring success. AI is a tool, not a replacement for the human elements crucial to the functioning of HR.

Chapter 7. Case Study Analysis: AI Innovators in HR

In recent years, innovators have taken giant strides in the realm of HR, revolutionizing traditional processes with the application of AI. The following sections will delve into some companies that have successfully integrated AI into their HR practices to various extents.

7.1. AI in Recruitment

Companies around the globe are consistently seeking to streamline their recruitment procedures. AI has presented a viable solution to achieve this end. Let's take a glimpse at two corporations that have embraced AI to enhance their hiring practices.

7.1.1. Case Study: Unilever

Traditional hiring practices are notably flawed, often leading to bias and unfavorable drops in diversity. Unilever has spearheaded novel adjustments to their hiring processes by implementing AI. The company employs online games to assess a candidate's aptitude and potential. Following this, Unilever utilizes HireVue, an AI tool, to conduct a video interview with candidates. The software analyzes facial movements, speech, and lexicon, judging the applicant's suitability for the specified role.

The integration of AI into Unilever's recruitment process has been overwhelmingly beneficial. HireVue's efficiency has reduced the hiring time from four months to four weeks. This period is a mere 10% of the previous time taken, a significant time and cost cut.

Moreover, use of such software has minimized human bias, making the process objective and equitable. As a result, the company has experienced a hike in workforce diversity, leading to a broad array of perspectives enriching their innovation and problem-solving capabilities.

7.1.2. Case Study: IBM

IBM, another company at the forefront of the AI adoption in HR, uses its AI recruiting solution, Watson Talent. IBM Watson can quickly process huge volumes of applications, eliminating subpar candidates and creating a shortlist of qualified individuals. This slick operation significantly decreases time consumed, freeing HR personnel to focus on other pivotal tasks.

Watson also endeavors to fine-tune job descriptions, ensuring these are attractive and inclusive, increasing the likelihood of drawing in a diverse and talented applicant pool.

7.2. Improving Employee Engagement

Machine learning algorithms can analyze employee behaviors, providing insights to improve engagement and increase productivity.

7.2.1. Case Study: Humu

Humu, a firm based in Mountain View, strives to "nudge" companies into shape. Predicated on Google's behavioral economic research, information is analyzed from systems like HRIS and email metadata to generate insights on team dynamics. Periodic "nudging" emails are sent to managers based on these insights, suggesting actionable steps towards improving team engagement and productivity.

The impact made by Humu's AI application is substantial. Client companies have recorded up to 10% upticks in retention enhancement, as well as noticeable improvements in team productivity.

7.3. AI in Employee's Learning and Development

Employee training and development is another area where companies are utilizing AI to produce remarkable returns.

7.3.1. Case Study: Infosys

Infosys, a global leader in next-generation digital services and consulting, has integrated an AI platform, known as Nia, into internal operations. Nia is a self-learning system that supports employees by providing recommendations on professional development. Infosys also employs an AI-based training portal, Lex, helping their global team keep apace with the evolving knowledge needed in their area of expertise.

Infosys' approach has resulted in a smoother, ongoing learning process, equipping employees with necessary competencies and ensuring they stay ahead of the curve. It has optimized both the training and up-skilling of employees, resulting in a more empowered workforce.

In conclusion, AI applications have permeated various phases of HR, from recruitment to employee engagement and learning and development. Companies like Unilever, IBM, Humu, and Infosys are leading the way, using AI to increase efficiency and equity in their HR processes. These implementations have demonstrated tangible results via saved time, increased productivity, and higher employee retention.

While AI's integration into HR offers phenomenal solutions, it is critical to remember that these technologies are tools to augment and not replace the human workforce. Therefore, companies should equip their HR departments to leverage AI benefits properly without diluting the human touch that will always be central to Human

Resources.

Chapter 1. Introduction

In our dynamic and ever-innovating world, the integration of Artificial Intelligence (AI) within the Human Resources (HR) sector is paving the way for monumental shifts in how businesses operate. This invaluable Special Report, titled "AI in Human Resources: Insights, Automation, and Personalization," unravels the complexities of this alliance, transforming technical jargon into friendly language that encourages understanding and inspires actionable change. Discover how AI is introducing more efficient automation processes, evolving data-driven insights, and crafting a more personalized HR experience. Despite veering into the highly technical territory of AI, we serve up this knowledge in an engaging, easy-to-grasp manner. So why wait? Equip yourself with this groundbreaking report and unlock the potential of AI in your HR department. Your journey towards a smarter HR begins here!

Chapter 2. The Dawn of AI in HR

Intrinsically, the coupling of Artificial Intelligence and Human Resources was a development waiting to happen. Ever since human resources became a defined segment in organizations, the onus has been on making the procedures more effective and error-free. The advent of AI has furnished us with an opportunity to supercharge these aspirations, driving HR into an era marked by increased productivity, pattern recognition, automation, and personalized experiences. To properly appreciate AI's impact, it is critical we detail its dawn in the HR realm.

2.1. The Inception of AI in HR

The story of AI's integration into HR began not too long ago. The initial steps began with self-learning algorithms and basic predictive analytics to improve efficiencies and automate simple tasks. These early systems could undertake administrative tasks, such as filing and sorting resumes or answering frequently asked questions from employees. The efficiency they offered was massive, which caused businesses to take notice.

Over time, AI matured and developed more advanced tools capable of supporting more complex responsibilities. Learning from their interactions with human beings, AI powered HR tech began to predict worker behaviors and even started providing useful insights that could improve the overall functioning of the HR department.

2.2. The Role of AI in Early HR Transformation

The prime motive behind AI's early adoption in HR was efficiency. HR departments are notorious for their administrative backend tasks, which are time-consuming yet essential. Machine learning and AI-driven automation tools found application in streamlining these processes, freeing HR professionals to concentrate on other critical tasks that contribute to strategic decision-making.

AI's initial capabilities were promptly realized with applications like resume parsing and automated responses. By doing the work of numerous employees in mere minutes, AI positioned itself as a vital entity in HR's growth and evolution.

2.3. Understanding AI's Role in Data Analysis

As AI evolved from its early days of mere automation, another facet of its potential began emerging - data analysis.

Human Resources tends to generate mountains of data, and AI has the capacity to sift through this information and identify patterns that humans may miss. It offers predictive analytics that can help forecast employee trends and behaviors, flag potential issues before they become significant problems, and even predict future hiring needs.

Using AI, HR departments can now utilize data to support decision-making, effectively marrying quantitative analysis with qualitative experiences to improve department efficiencies.

2.4. Personalizing the Employee Experience with AI

The final piece of the AI and HR puzzle lies in the personalization of the employee experience. AI's ability to facilitate contextual conversations and interactions allowed HR departments to offer personalized service to their employees. With chatbots, employees could get instantaneous, personalized information about their concerns or inquiries.

Moreover, workspace platforms powered by AI began predicting employee needs even before they articulated them, thereby aligning the available resources in alignment with the employees' expectations.

As AI continues to improve, it promises to further refine and redefine the HR department. However, despite AI's evident progress and potential, it also introduces a novel set of challenges related to reliance, ethics, and privacy.

2.5. The Challenges AI Brings to HR

The application of AI within HR is not without concerns. To start with, there is the reliance issue. What happens if the AI platform fails or develops a fault? Can businesses risk interruptions?

The ethical issues surrounding bias in AI decision-making is another critical area. Even though AI can streamline processes and sift through data effectively, it can also inadvertently reinforce existing biases if not correctly programmed.

Moreover, concerns around privacy rights and the use of employee data by AI systems are an ongoing conversation, which will need to be addressed with robust guidelines, laws, and regulations over time.

Chapter 8. Overcoming Challenges: The Roadblocks to AI Adoption in HR

Integration of artificial intelligence (AI) into the Human Resources (HR) sector harbors immense potential for operational efficiency and personalized user experience. However, the journey towards these beneficial outcomes is marked by roadblocks and challenges. The next segment delves into these obstacles and provides potential solutions to facilitate smoother adoption of AI in HR.

8.1. Understanding the AI Landscape

The term AI often conjures images of complex algorithms, high-tech robotics, and an overwhelming technological landscape that is difficult to navigate. This perception often deters HR professionals, breeding fear and uncertainty that hinder the adoption of AI in HR.

To overcome this challenge, it is essential to educate and empower HR teams about the fundamentals and applications of AI. Webinars, workshops, tech talks, and online courses can help demystify AI, fostering a more comfortable and transparent relationship with the technology. Such initiatives also encourage curiosity and critical thinking, essential traits in an AI-driven environment.

8.2. Handling Data Responsibly

Data is the fuel that powers AI, and ensuring its responsible management is crucial. However, concerns of data privacy, security, and unethical use present a significant challenge to AI adoption.

Handling sensitive employee data responsibly requires stringent data management policies, adherence to data protection laws, and secure data storage systems. The HR department must also be transparent with employees about what data is being collected, why it's collected, and how it's used.

8.3. The Infrastructural Overhaul

Another challenge lies in the infrastructural changes required to support AI solutions. This often involves significant investment in hardware, software, and training. For smaller companies and those with limited resources, this could prove prohibitive.

To address this, companies can explore cost-effective AI platforms that offer scalable solutions. Adopting a phased approach to AI integration can also spread out the financial impact. An initial small-scale rollout could provide insights into the necessary changes and investments required for a complete overhaul.

8.4. Championing Employee Acceptance

A common fear among employees is that AI will replace human jobs, making them redundant. This perception forms a significant barrier to AI adoption in HR.

To address this, it's essential to clarify that AI is less about replacing human effort and more about augmenting it. HR should clearly communicate that the primary role of AI is to handle mundane tasks, freeing up HR professionals to focus on tasks requiring human touch and judgment. This new narrative can help foster acceptance.

8.5. The Skills Gap

A significant challenge to implementing AI in HR is the current skills gap. Finding talent with the right balance of HR knowledge and AI expertise is difficult.

Closing this skills gap will require both internal training programs and external hires. Internally, companies could foster an environment of continuous learning and skills development. Externally, they could look into collaborative efforts with educational institutions or AI providers.

8.6. Ensuring Ethical and Unbiased AI

AI applications can unintentionally perpetuate bias if diverse datasets do not train them. This poses a challenge as biased AI can lead to unfair HR practices.

Investing in bias-detection tools and promoting diverse and inclusive data sets can help counteract this. Additionally, cultivating transparency and allowing employees access to their AI-generated data and insights could encourage trust in the AI systems.

8.7. Measuring AI Success

Finally, companies must grapple with how to measure AI's impact on HR. This is important for assessing ROI and making future strategy decisions.

Defining metrics that capture both quantitative and qualitative changes brought about by AI can help address this issue. Such metrics might cover time saved, reduced manual errors, improved employee engagement, and feedback from HR staff and employees.

In summary, while the road towards AI adoption in HR is filled with challenges, understanding these obstacles can guide effective strategies to navigate them. Indeed, in the alliance of AI and HR, acknowledging and overcoming these roadblocks is key to unlocking the immense potential of AI in transforming HR practices. By embarking on this journey, companies stand to gain from improved efficiency, increased accuracy, and a digital-first approach that revolutionizes HR functions.

Chapter 9. Regulatory Landscape: Ethics and Compliance in AI-Infused HR

The integration of AI within HR calls for a nuanced understanding of the regulatory landscape. Industry standards, legal implications, ethical considerations, and compliance measures comprise the foundation of this vast terrain. This scope is not only essential for responsible AI use but also instrumental in circumnavigating potential pitfalls and leveraging AI for optimal impact, effectiveness, and fairness.

9.1. Compliance with Laws and Regulation

First and foremost, aligning AI application with legal and regulatory frameworks is paramount. Companies need to adhere to local, regional, and global laws that regulate data management, speech recognition, analytics, or any area that AI technology might touch upon. Similarly, employment laws should be considered when it comes to AI employment screening or worker surveillance. Ensuring that all AI propositions are in line with the General Data Protection Regulation (GDPR) and other global data privacy laws is crucial. Organizations must remain aware of these regulations to avoid hefty penalties, reputational damage, and lost consumer confidence.

Laws governing data management and privacy are especially significant given the vast amount of data that AI systems need for operations. As AI becomes more refined and more businesses begin to integrate it into their human resources practices, the legal landscape will undoubtedly become more sophisticated, requiring compliance activities to be proactive and ongoing.

9.2. Ethical Considerations

Ethics serves as a cornerstone of AI implementation and offers a prism through which to view AI's broader social implications. While regulations and laws provide a statutory framework for AI use, ethics weigh the moral implications of AI implementations, considering factors such as inclusivity, transparency, interpretability, and fairness.

Fairness in AI ensures that it operates without bias or discrimination—a critical matter in HR, especially during the hiring process. HR departments must ensure that AI isn't beneficial to one demographic at the expense of others, perpetuating inequities. AI systems must be audited regularly to detect, mitigate, or eliminate bias.

Transparency pertains to the clarity of AI underpinnings—the algorithms beneath the application. While it may not be viable for everyone in the HR department to understand the complex workings of AI, it is essential that there is a degree of transparency regarding how decisions are made. In turn, this fuels interpretability, the right to an explanation of why and how AI came to a particular decision or recommendation.

Similarly, the inclusion principle suggests that AI implementation in HR should consider a diverse range of individuals and circumstances, ensuring the application of AI technology does not drastically marginalize or exclude any group.

9.3. Navigating Algorithmic Bias

A significant offshoot of ethical considerations is the challenge of algorithmic bias. Algorithms are programmed by humans, which can lead to unintentional biases based on racial, gender, or other sociological criteria. To tackle this, it's essential to have a diverse team of developers that can bring varied perspectives to the table during the development stage. Data sets used to train machines should also be diverse and comprehensive, allowing the AI system to operate with reduced bias.

AI system testing should be thorough, with rigorous measures to investigate potential biases hidden within the system or its operations. By putting effective mitigation strategies in place, organizations can minimize bias and ensure the AI system responds impartially across diverse groups.

9.4. Security Measures

Security is paramount when dealing with AI in an HR context. As AI systems process large volumes of data, including sensitive personal information, the risk of data breaches increases exponentially. Strong encryption and secure data storage solutions are necessary, and HR departments need adequate cybersecurity measures to protect against cyber threats.

9.5. Employees' Rights and Trust

The integration of AI into HR should be accompanied by building trust among employees. Employees have a right to understand how their data is being used and for what purpose. Clear communication about data collection, storage, and usage practices will encourage trust and minimize resistance to AI technology. The adoption of 'privacy by design' principles may also help to ensure that privacy considerations are built into AI systems from the outset.

Organizations must also be aware of the effect of AI on employees' mental well-being. The impact of surveillance measures or performance analytics on stress, productivity, and overall job satisfaction must be delicately balanced with the potential benefits of these technologies. Regular reviews, employee feedback, and remediation measures should be in place to manage these outcomes.

The Regulatory landscape for AI-infused HR is a complex but navigable terrain. A balance of law and ethics, intertwined with a commitment to fairness, transparency, security, and employee trust, paves the way for more responsible and effective AI implementation. As businesses continue to embrace AI in their HR practices, adapting to the ebb and flow of this landscape is a journey, not a destination.

Chapter 10. Future Projections: The Role of HR in an AI-Dominant World

As we peer into the magnifying glass of the future and contemplate the escalating role of AI, it's indisputable that HR workflows will face fundamental transformations. Traces of these monumental changes are already rippling through both colossal corporations and nimble startups.

10.1. A Shift Towards AI-Driven HR Processes

In traditional HR, most of the tasks involved paperwork and manual labor. Timesheets, leaves, benefits, and payroll required HR professionals to be encircled by paperwork. With AI stepping onto the scene, such routine tasks are automated, freeing up HR personnel to invest their time into more strategic roles like employee engagement or leadership development.

Automation, however, doesn't stop at administrative duties. Hiring processes are likewise feeling the AI impact. By integrating AI in automatic resume screening, HR teams can shortlist candidates faster and more efficiently, based on specific criteria. Combined with predictive analytics, AI could significantly enhance HR's capabilities in talent acquisition and retention.

10.2. Unleashing the Power of Data

With the power to process vast volumes of data, AI provides HR with powerful insights. Being able to collect and interpret employee data across multiple domains – engagement, performance, attrition, and others – can craft a comprehensive picture of the workforce. With AI-driven analytics, organizations can utilize predictive modeling to anticipate employee turnover, boost engagement, identify skill gaps, and much more. The use of such data can drive better decision-making and a more strategic approach to HR.

Furthermore, AI has substantial implications in improving HR analytics. Conventional HR data tools look at simple, linear relationships and single factors. In contrast, AI can weave together complex, multifaceted data and reveal profound insights that shape more informed decisions.

10.3. Personalization in HR: A New Norm

The infusion of AI in HR isn't merely about speed and efficiency. It's also about customizing the HR experience for each individual. AI can help HR leaders to gain a deep understanding of what motivates each employee, better manage talent, and deliver what they need to perform at their best, thus optimising productivity.

AI, combined with big data analytics, can create "employee personas" – detailed profiles of employee behavior based on vast amounts of varied data. From working styles to preferred modes of communication, these personas can allow HR teams to address the unique needs of each employee, propelling workplace satisfaction.

10.4. Ethical Considerations In An AI-Dominant HR World

Every massive leap forward necessitates responsible governance, and AI in HR is no exception. In view of the mass data collection that powers AI, critical conversations should be commenced regarding data privacy, transparency, and fairness.

AI applications in HR must be considerate of existing ethical standards and legislation. For instance, maintaining the anonymity of employee data, avoiding over-reliance on machine-generated recommendations without human verification, and ensuring that AI is not contributing to unfair bias in recruitment or performance assessments are some aspects that require careful scrutiny.

10.5. Preparing for an AI-Fuelled Future

HR's metamorphosis into an AI-driven practice is still underway, making it vital for HR professionals to ready themselves for adapting to these new technologies. Future-proofing HR skillsets will no longer be optional; it will be essential for survival in this swiftly progressing era of AI.

Emphasis should be placed on continuously enhancing digital literacy and analytical capabilities among HR professionals. Equally important is fostering an innovative mindset to creatively apply AI-empowered insights in building human-centric solutions within the workplace.

In conclusion, the integration of AI will significantly reshape HR functions and redefine roles within the department. While the transition may be challenging, the opportunities are potent enough to transform HR into an even more strategic arm within organizations. The fusion of artificial and human intelligence will usher in a brave new world for HR. AI is not poised to replace the human touch in HR but rather amplify it, making HR more insightful, efficient, and personalized than ever before.

Chapter 11. Final Thoughts: Preparing Your HR for the AI Revolution

In the preceding chapters, we unraveled the vast expanse of the AI landscape and the tremendous transformation it is triggering in the HR sector. We navigated through the terminologies, techniques, and potential applications. We also debriefed on the challenges, opportunities and ethics associated with AI integration. Now, it's time to knuckle down and revisit our fundamentals before gearing up for the AI revolution.

11.1. Building AI-ready Infrastructure

To support the integration of AI tools, it's critical that your organization's infrastructure is well-equipped and responsive. Preparation is key: you need to ensure your databases, servers, data storage systems, and network capabilities are up to the task of handling the influx of information.

Invest in systems that allow for seamless synchronizing and sharing of data across multiple HR functions. Prioritize security to protect the data your AI tools will be working with. Also, remember to frequently back up your data to ensure that it's protected against potential failures or cyber threats.

11.2. Embracing a Data-Driven Culture

The decision-making process within your HR must be transformed from a traditional approach to being data-driven. Data literacy should be a basic competence for all your employees, not just for the IT department. It's essential to create a culture within your organization where decisions are based on facts and analytical reasoning, rather than pure instinct or one-off experiences.

This transformation does not happen overnight. Begin with training your HR team on the basics of the data, its value, management, interpretation, and governance. Make data a part of everyday conversations and decisions. Encourage sharing and democratisation of information and foster a sense of curiosity and critical thinking among your staff.

11.3. Establish Strong Ethics and Governance Policies

AI introduces a set of ethical and legal challenges to HR. Transparency, privacy, and accountability form the three pillars for ethical AI.

Any AI system used in HR should be transparent and explainable. Employees have a right to know how decisions about them are being made. All AI systems should follow strict privacy laws to protect employee information and to ensure there is no bias within the system. Finally, accountability in AI systems is crucial. In case of failures, it must be clear who is responsible.

Formulating an AI ethics policy within the organization is of utmost importance. The policy should write out the ethical guidelines, the data privacy strategy, and how to handle potential errors or bias. Regular audits and compliance checks should be conducted to ensure adherence to these standards.

11.4. Prepare Leadership for AI

Integrating AI into HR is not just a technological change, but also a leadership challenge. AI-influenced decision-making will call for adjustments in leadership style and thinking. Leaders must understand the potential of AI, be open to changes, and set up a learning culture to utilize the technology in the best way possible.

Being progressive and a lifelong learner should be an integral part of your leadership's vision. Encourage them to undergo AI and digital literacy courses to understand and manage the changes AI would bring.

11.5. Rolling Out a Robust Training Program

Lastly, but perhaps most importantly, prepare your entire HR department and the wider organization for the integration of AI. This involves rolling out a robust training program to equip everyone with the skills needed to utilize and manage AI.

The training program could include elements of data literacy, basic coding, using AI software and data protection. Personalize each person's training program to fit their specific role within the organization. Remember, as much as AI is about technology, it is also about people.

There is no denying the impact that the AI revolution will have on the world of HR. It is expected to bring in increased efficiency, data-driven insights, and better personalization of the HR experience. However, the real success in this transition lies in understanding the repercussions of AI, preparing your organization accordingly, and then taking the plunge.

AI has the potential to do more than automate tasks - it can enhance human capabilities, build relationships, and create a more fulfilling, productive workplace environment. However, we must tread this path with caution, ethical awareness, and an acute understanding of the tools we wield.

As your organization journeys towards a smarter HR, remember to keep your human roles in view, even as we step into this brave new world of artificial intelligence. This balance is what will enable us to make the best use of AI in HR.